EARTHSHAKING

NATURAL DISASTERS!

D1509044

Chana Stiefel

Steck-Vaughn

A Harcourt Achieve Imprint

www.Steck-Vaughn.com
1-800-531-5015

Earthshaking Natural Disasters!
By Chana Stiefel

Photo Acknowledgements
Cover ©Digital Vision/Getty Images/HA Collection; t.o.c. ©SENA
VIDANAGAMA/AFP/Getty Images; p. 5 ©Will & Deni McIntyre/Photo
Researchers, Inc.; p. 7 ©Joseph Sohm; ChromoSohm Inc./CORBIS; p. 9
©Gary Hincks/Science Photo Library; p. 13 ©ROMEO GACAD/AFP/
Getty Images; p. 15 ©SENA VIDANAGAMA/AFP/Getty Images; p.
18–19 Illustration by NOAA via Getty Images; p. 20 ©DPA/The Image
Works; p. 23 ©STF/AFP/Getty Images; p. 25 ©Dorling Kindersley/
Getty Images; p. 27 ©UNEP/Topham/The Image Works; p. 28 © Helena
Buurman.

ISBN 1-4190-2281-4

Printed in China
3 4 5 6 7 8 788 12 11 10 09 08 07

Table of Contents

Extreme Makeover
Earth Edition

You're riding your bike down the street. There's blue sky overhead. A gentle breeze blows in your hair. Suddenly, the pavement starts to shake. The sidewalk snaps like a potato chip. Trees fall. Windows shatter. Then, within seconds, the **tremors** stop. The shake-up leaves a trail of damage. What on Earth is going on?

You've just lived through an **earthquake**. It's a reminder that the earth is not just a solid ball of rock. Under the surface, it's moving and changing. These changes can cause major disasters. They can strike deep under the sea or on dry land.

In this book, you'll read about three kinds of earth-shattering events: earthquakes, huge waves called **tsunamis**, and the eruption of **volcanoes**. You'll visit the scenes of the disasters. You'll learn how they happen. You'll see how well science can predict when the next event will strike. Find out more about our amazing planet. Read on!

Earthquakes

Quake-Up Time

It was 4:31 A.M. on January 17, 1994. Eunice Glassberg was jolted awake. Her home in Woodland Hills, California, was trembling violently. "The floor and walls were shaking and swaying," she recalls.

Glassberg leaped out of bed. She grabbed her four children. It was still dark. They ran for a doorway between the kitchen and the dining room. The house felt like it might crumble. If it did, she hoped the frame of the door would protect them.

The worst shaking lasted only a minute. "It was the longest minute of my life," Glassberg says. "Everything fell out of my kitchen cabinets. My grandfather clock fell and smashed."

For three hours, smaller tremors shook the house. They're called **aftershocks**. The family stayed in the doorway the entire time. "It was like a scary ride that had no end," Glassberg recalls. "We were paralyzed with fear."

The Glassbergs had survived one of the worst earthquakes in U.S. history.

This earthquake did more than $40 billion worth of damage. ▶
It struck in Northridge, California. Northridge is 6.5 kilometers
(4 miles) from the Glassberg's home. The area is part of Los Angeles.
It's one of the largest cities in the United States.

The quake killed 57 people. It left nearly 12,000 more injured. It damaged or destroyed about 12,500 buildings. Seven highway bridges collapsed. Water and sewage pipes burst. Gas lines exploded. Over 2.5 million homes lost electric power.

Fault Zone

What caused so much damage? Picture the earth as a giant peach. The "pit" is Earth's solid inner core. The "juicy" middle part is the **mantle**. This layer is mostly made of molten, or nearly melted, rock. Earth's outer "skin" is made of a hard, rocky **crust**.

The crust is made of large slabs of rock called **tectonic plates**. (See page 9.) The plates float on the earth's soft upper mantle. Most earthquakes happen along tectonic plate boundaries.

How do earthquakes develop? Tectonic plates are always moving. They slide past each other. As they move, the rough edges of the plates rub against each other. Sometimes they stick. The plates try to move, but they can't. Enormous stress builds in the rock. To relieve the **pressure**, the rock bends. Sometimes, the rock will break and form a **fault**. If the pressure gets too strong, the rocks along the fault slide suddenly past each other. A huge amount of energy is released. That sudden jolt of energy is an earthquake.

Tectonic Action

Most earthquakes happen along fault lines like those in this map.
These are the edges of Earth's tectonic plates. Volcanoes also appear
along these edges. Can you guess why? Find out in Chapter 3.

Hundreds of faults lie under California. Most are well mapped. Still, everyone was surprised by the Los Angeles quake. The fault lay hidden about 15 kilometers (9.3 miles) underground.

The quake struck under the town of Northridge. The Glassberg's home was just a short distance away. The spot underground where the rocks suddenly snapped is called the **focus**. During an earthquake, **vibrations** spread out from the focus. They travel as **seismic waves**. (See page 11.) These energy waves move in all directions. They make the ground shake, rise, and fall. Buildings may crumble. Highways can crack. The worst damage usually happens right above the earthquake's focus.

Scientists can measure the strength of an earthquake. They use an instrument called a **seismograph**. It measures how much an earthquake shakes the ground. The strength of an earthquake is called its **magnitude**. It's often charted on the Richter scale. The Richter scale assigns numbers to each earthquake. A magnitude 8.0 quake is 10 times as strong as a magnitude 7.0. It is 100 times the strength of a magnitude 6.0 quake.

Today, more than 8,000 stations around the world measure earthquakes. How many do they record? Several *million* earthquakes rock our planet every year. Most are very small. Many happen in out-of-the-way places.

Do the Wave

When an earthquake strikes, it sends energy through the planet. The energy travels in waves. There are three main kinds of seismic waves.

P Waves (primary waves)

These are the fastest waves. They compress and expand the ground. Think of a spring toy being squeezed and then stretched. That's what P waves do.

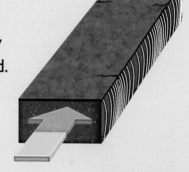

S Waves (secondary waves)

S Waves are next on the scene. They move more slowly in a snakelike motion. They shake the earth from side to side.

Surface Waves

When waves reach the surface of the earth, they're called surface waves. These waves do the most damage. They make the ground rise and fall. They also shake it from side to side.

Major earthquakes (7 to 7.9 on the Richter scale) happen about 17 times a year. The Northridge quake scored a 6.7 on the Richter scale. It is considered major because it happened in one of the busiest places in the world.

Forecast: Rumbles and Shakes

Earthquakes usually strike without warning. For decades, scientists have tried to predict them. They set up seismographs to record rumblings. They use satellites to measure tiny shifts near fault lines.

Still, scientists have failed to predict a major quake. They can only tell us how likely it is that one will happen. For example, the San Francisco Bay lies near a fault line. Scientists say an earthquake may strike there sometime in the next 30 years. The chances are 62 percent. In Southern California, the chances are 60 percent.

How do these predictions help? For starters, they help people to prepare. City planners can build safer buildings, bridges, and highways. Town officials can set up emergency plans. Residents can stock up on fresh water and batteries. Schools can run earthquake-safety drills. Finally, people can move out of the area if they want.

After the Northridge quake, the Glassbergs made a tough choice. The whole family decided to move back east. On moving day, another earthquake struck. It convinced the Glassbergs that they were doing the right thing. As Eunice Glassberg said, "I'm better prepared to deal with blizzards."

Seismographs measure and record seismic activity in the ground. The lines represent the waves of an earthquake.

Tsunamis

Waves of Destruction

Koshi Mackenroe John was 13 years old. He lived on a small island in the Indian Ocean. His tribe numbered about 30,000 people. They raised pigs, and they grew coconuts, yams, and bananas. They lived and played on beautiful beaches.

Then, without warning, Koshi's world was swept away. It happened on December 26, 2004. Huge waves suddenly struck his island. Koshi, his parents, and his sister scrambled to safety on a hilltop. The water destroyed everything around them.

Suddenly, they were homeless. They had little food. All Koshi could do was wait—and write letters. He had saved a notebook. Now, he filled its pages with pleas for help.

On December 26, 2004, the coastlines of the Indian Ocean experienced a devastating tsunami. It created waves up to 30 meters (99 feet) tall. Many survivors were left homeless and hungry.

"Dear Uncle," he wrote on December 28. "I hope you will find this letter very soon. . . . We need an immediate rescue. We are starving over here and trying to send messages. . . . Everything is over and devastated. . . . From the west side only water and water can be seen. . . . There is no sign of land."

Sadly, Koshi's story is only one of millions. The disaster he described was the most destructive tsunami in recorded history. A tsunami is a series of huge waves. This one was caused by an undersea earthquake. It struck 12 countries in Asia and Africa. Walls of water crashed into coastlines. Some of them were 9 to 30 meters (30 to 100 feet) high. More than 200,000 people were killed. About 5 million others were left homeless. Many had no food or clothing.

Undersea Explosion

Where did this watery monster come from? It began off the coast of Sumatra. It was 7:58 A.M. A magnitude 9.0 earthquake struck beneath the ocean floor. It was more than 100 times the size of the Northridge quake. The vibrations caused trillions of tons of sea water to rise and fall in a few seconds. Waves spread out in all directions. They traveled about 800 kilometers (500 miles) per hour. That's as fast as a jet plane.

At first, tsunami waves are hard to notice. The sea is so deep that the waves seem small. They reach only 1 to 2 meters (3 to 6 feet) above sea level. They are also very spread out. The distance from wave to wave can be more than 160 kilometers (100 miles). The distance from one wave to the next is called the **wavelength**. Initially, these waves traveled 10 to 20 minutes apart.

Wave Action

Here's how the tsunami developed:

1 Waves formed after an earthquake occurred on the sea floor. In the deep water, their wavelength was extremely long. Wavelength is measured from crest (highest point) to crest.

2 The waves neared the shore. They hit the shallow sea floor. That slowed them down. The waves bunched together. The **compression** made the height, or **amplitude**, of the waves grow. Some waves reached as high as five-story buildings.

3 Walls of water crashed into shore. Flooding stretched up to 2 kilometers (1.25 miles) inland. Buildings collapsed. People were thrown into trees. Then, the water rushed back. It swept cars, boats, and people out to sea.

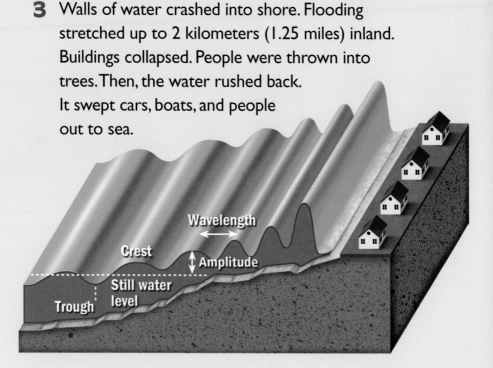

Wavelength

Crest

Amplitude

Still water level

Trough

The first wave slammed into Banda Aceh (BAHN-duh AH-chay) in Sumatra 15 minutes after the earthquake. It surged over land. It crushed buildings. It tossed ships around like toys in a bathtub. Thousands of people drowned. Within 7 hours, waves had even reached east Africa. That's about 4,800 kilometers (3,000 miles) from where the earthquake occured. (See maps below.)

Tsunami Alert!

After the disaster, everyone had the same question: *Why wasn't there any warning?* After all, scientists can often predict tsunamis. In many parts of the world, **sensors** are placed under the sea. These devices measure the **factors** that lead to a tsunami. The sensors detect earthquakes. They also sense changes in wave height.

The waves started just off the coast of Sumatra.

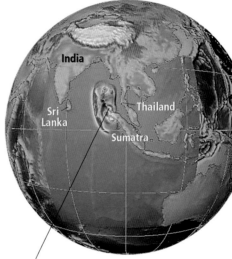

Within minutes, giant waves hit the coasts of Sumatra and Thailand.

If the sensors detect an earthquake, an alert is sent to nearby floating **buoys**. The buoys send the data to a warning center. Then, government officials warn the public. They send out radio broadcasts. They set off alarms. Even a five-minute warning can help. It gives people time to run for higher ground.

Sadly, the Indian Ocean didn't have a warning system in 2004. Tsunamis don't happen there very often. In 1883, the last devastating tsunami hit the area. It followed the eruption of Krakatoa, an Indonesian volcano. Since then, only one tsunami had developed in the Indian Ocean.

About 85 percent of all tsunamis happen in the Pacific Ocean. There, tectonic plates jam together. They cause a high number of earthquakes. Between 1900 and 2001, 796 tsunamis struck the Pacific. At least 9 of them caused serious damage. Today, a warning system in the Pacific Ocean helps save lives.

The waves rapidly spread through the Indian Ocean.

In less than two hours, the waves reached India and Sri Lanka.

Help Wanted

After the 2004 tsunami, victims needed help. They were left without food, homes, or clothing. People around the world raised money for the victims. About $10 billion was sent to the region. It will help build new homes, schools, and businesses.

Hopefully, some of that money will help Koshi Mackenroe John. He and his family waited on that island hilltop for several days. He kept writing letters. Finally, two of them were delivered to his uncle. Government officials also received copies. Soon, the family was rescued by ship. They were taken to a relief camp. There, life would begin again for them, as it would for so many others.

People around the world responded to the tsunami tragedy by sending money, food, medicine, water, and supplies.

Students to the Rescue

Between one-third and one-half of the tsunami victims were children. Many more children became orphans. Kids around the world came up with creative ways to help.

- A Connecticut high school held a "dress down" day. Students paid a dollar to wear pajama bottoms to school. Teachers paid $5 to wear jeans. The event raised more than $3,000 for tsunami relief.

- In Winchester, Kentucky, kids dressed up. They held a "Crazy Dress-Up Day." Students donated a dollar or more. Then, they got to wear crazy costumes to school.

- One class in California sold "tsunami awareness ribbons." They raised more than $2,600.

- A class in Massachusetts recycled more than 5,600 bottles. They collected about $300 for tsunami relief.

- Kids in Tennessee started a "Tsunami Sole-Mate Project." They collected more than 3,000 pairs of shoes in a week. A local church shipped them to tsunami victims.

CHAPTER 3

Volcanoes

A Mountain Awakes

The town of Armero lay at the foot of Colombia's Andes Mountains. Farmers grew crops of white rice and cotton on the mountainside. They called Armero the "White City."

A huge volcano loomed over the town. Its name was Nevado del Ruiz (neh-VAH-doe del roo-EES). The people, though, paid little attention to it. Nevado del Ruiz had been **dormant** for more than 140 years. Its cap was covered in snow.

Then, on the night of November 13, 1985, everything changed. Nevado del Ruiz erupted. Hot ash, rocks, and gas shot from the top of the mountain. The heat melted the snow and ice. Floods of water rushed down the volcano. The speeding water picked up rocks and soil. The rivers flooded. Huge mudflows called **lahars** (LAH-hars) poured into Armero.

The lahars moved like rivers of wet cement. They had the strength to uproot trees. They could lift houses off the ground. As they traveled, the lahars grew in size and speed. They were 40 meters (130 feet) thick. They flowed downhill at 60 kilometers (37.2 miles) per hour.

This is Armero, Columbia, after the eruption of Nevado del Ruiz in 1985. A pilot flew over the town. "Armero has disappeared from the map," he said.

It was 11:30 P.M. Most of Armero's 28,000 villagers were sleeping. Without warning, the lahars came crashing into town. Nearly all of the buildings were either swept away or buried. The destruction only took 10 or 20 minutes. More than 23,000 people were killed. About 5,000 more residents were badly injured.

Kaboom!

Today, there are about 1,500 active volcanoes in the world. More than 50 of them erupt every year.

What lies inside these fiery mountains? The mantle under the earth's crust is super hot. Temperatures rise as high as 4,000° C (7,232° F). Earth's tectonic plates move above the mantle. When two plates collide, the lower one may sink into the mantle. The heat **transforms** the plate's rock into a thick, boiling liquid called **magma**.

Magma is less dense than solid rock. Because of this, magma rises up through Earth's crust. As more and more magma builds up, the pressure increases. It needs to escape. Then—BOOM!—it bursts out onto the surface. When the red, fiery magma hits the surface, it's called **lava**.

How a Volcano Erupts

Inside a volcano, heat and pressure push upward. In some volcanoes, **vents** form and lava leaks out slowly over long periods of time. In others, the magma and gases are trapped. There are not enough vents to release the pressure. It's like when boiling water rattles the lid of a pot. Finally, the pressure grows too great and the volcano blows its top. An eruption like this can be as powerful as an atomic bomb!

Lava

Vents

Magma

Want to see a volcano in action? Head for the Pacific. Volcanoes and earthquakes tend to happen in that part of the world. In fact, a big circle around the Pacific Ocean is called the "Ring of Fire."

Many of the earth's tectonic plates meet at the Ring of Fire. The colliding plates help create lots of molten rock. Over millions of years, this magma rises. It flows out of the sea floor or ground as lava. The lava hardens as it cools back into rock. That rock eventually forms a volcanic mountain. That is exactly how Nevado del Ruiz was created.

Warning Signs

The disaster in Armero wasn't a complete surprise. Nevado del Ruiz had been "restless." Scientists had recorded warning signs. They noticed many small earthquakes. The amount of gas trapped in the volcano had increased. Sometimes steam burst through the mountain top.

Before the eruption, scientists tried to help people prepare. They **determined** where the lahars would flow. They drew maps. Communities near the volcano were warned, but few people took action. The government didn't order people to leave. They didn't want to cause trouble with a false alarm.

Mount Pinatubo in the Philippines erupted in 1991. This time, people were prepared. Scientists knew that magma was rising and that pressure was building. The government acted just in time. They evacuated about 60,000 people before the eruption.

Today, about 500 million people around the world live near a volcano. When will the next one blow? Scientists aren't sure, but they're learning the warning signs from past eruptions. Today, predicting eruptions isn't the biggest problem. It's convincing people to leave their homes when the time comes.

Volcano Lover

Meet Seth Moran. He's a volcanologist (a scientist who studies volcanoes) at the Cascades Volcano Observatory in Vancouver, Washington. Would you want his job?

Hi, Seth. Describe your typical day.

I start my day at my computer. I look at seismic data. We have instruments on 13 volcanoes. We measure earthquakes and other activity. About two or three times a year, we go into the field. We set up or repair our instruments. Sometimes they get damaged in small eruptions.

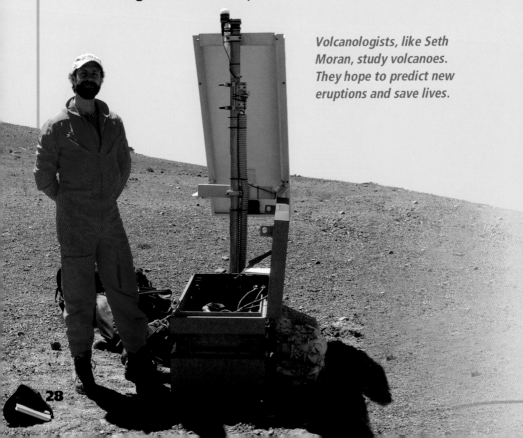

Volcanologists, like Seth Moran, study volcanoes. They hope to predict new eruptions and save lives.

What does your seismic data tell you?

Earthquakes are the best signs of an eruption. Sometimes they get bigger and happen more often. Then there's a good chance that an eruption is about to happen.

Have you ever had a scary experience?

In November 2004, we went to Mount St. Helens [in Washington]. We were a quarter mile from the vent. Steam bursts starting coming up. We returned to our helicopter. A poof of ash came toward us. We got out of there quickly.

So, this job can be dangerous?

Some volcanologists have died in eruptions. The place where I work is named after David Johnson. He was a scientist killed in the big eruption of Mount St. Helens in 1980.

When did you first become interested in volcanoes?

As a kid I loved volcanoes. I glued pictures of them into a scrapbook. In 1974, I was in second grade. My parents took me on a trip to Iceland. A volcano had erupted there. Lava was cutting off the harbor of this fishing village. The villagers took out fire hoses. They sprayed the lava to cool it down. They saved the town. Seeing the steaming lava left an impression on me.

What's the best part of the job?

It's lots of fun to watch the earth move.

Glossary

aftershock *(noun)* movement after an earthquake

amplitude *(noun)* the height of a wave

buoy *(noun)* an object floating in water to show a safe route or to warn of danger

compression *(noun)* the act of squeezing together

crust *(noun)* Earth's outer layer

determine *(verb)* to decide something; to make up one's mind

dormant *(adjective)* not active at the present time

earthquake *(noun)* the vibration of the ground caused by Earth's crust moving along faults

factor *(noun)* something that helps to produce a result

fault *(noun)* a break in Earth's crust

focus *(noun)* the place underground where an earthquake begins

lahar *(noun)* a mudflow caused by an eruption

lava *(noun)* molten rock that reaches the surface

magma *(noun)* molten rock beneath Earth's surface

magnitude *(noun)* greatness in size

mantle *(noun)* the thickest layer of the earth

pressure *(noun)* the force produced by one thing pushing against another

seismic wave *(noun)* an energy wave that makes the ground shake during an earthquake

seismograph *(noun)* an instrument that records earthquakes

sensor *(noun)* a device that measures changes

tectonic plate *(noun)* a section of Earth's crust

transform *(verb)* to change something's shape or appearance

tremor *(noun)* a shaking or trembling

tsunami *(noun)* a huge ocean wave caused by an undersea earthquake

vent *(noun)* the opening in a volcano through which lava and ash escape

vibration *(noun)* a rapid back and forth movement

volcano *(noun)* an opening in Earth's crust through which melted rock and steam escape

wavelength *(noun)* the distance between two waves

Idioms

paralyzed with fear *(page 6)* so scared you can't move
The scary movie had me paralyzed with fear.

Index